Relativel, ...ng

Relatively Speaking
Poems of Person and Place

Chip Dameron
&
Betsy Joseph

LITERARY PRESS
LAMAR UNIVERSITY

ISBN: 978-1-942956-96-9
LOC: 2022938085

Editor: Jennifer Do
Cover Photo: Glenn Carrie

Lamar University Literary Press
Beaumont, TX

In memory of our parents, Charles and Madge Dameron, whose gifts of curiosity and wonder continue to inspire us

Recent Poetry from Lamar University Literary Press

Lisa Adams, *Xuai*
Walter Bargen, *My Other Mother's Red Mercedes*
Jerry Bradley, *Collapsing into Possibility*
Mark Busby, *Through Our Times*
Julie Chappell, *Mad Habits of a Life*
Stan Crawford, *Resisting Gravity*
Glover Davis, *My Cap of Darkness*
William Virgil Davis, *The Bones Poems*
Jeffrey DeLotto, *Voices Writ in Sand*
Chris Ellery, *Elder Tree*
Dede Fox, *On Wings of Silence*
Alan Gann, *That's Entertainment*
Larry Griffin, *Cedar Plums*
Michelle Hartman, *Irony and Irrelevance*
Katherine Hoerth, *Goddess Wears Cowboy Boots*
Michael Jennings, *Crossings: A Record of Travel*
Gretchen Johnson, *A Trip Through Downer, Minnesota*
Betsy Joseph, *Only So Many Autumns*
Ulf Kirchdorfer, *Chewing Green Leaves*
Jim McGarrah, *A Balancing Act*
J. Pittman McGehee, *Nod of Knowing*
Laurence Musgrove, *Bluebonnet Sutras*
Benjamin Myers, *Black Sunday*
Janice Northerns, *Some Electric Hum*
Godspower Oboido, *Wandering Feet on Pebbled Shores*
Moumin Quizi, *Migratory Words*
Jan Seale, *The Parkinson Poems*
Steven Schroeder, *the moon, not the finger, pointing*
Glen Sorestad, *Hazards of Eden*
Vincent Spina, *The Sumptuous Hills of Gulfport*
W.K. Stratton, *Betrayal Creek*
Wally Swist, *Invocation*
Ken Waldman, *Sports Page*
Loretta Diane Walker, *Ode to My Mother's Voice*
Dan Williams, *Past Purgatory, a Distant Paradise*
Jonas Zdanys, *The Angled Road*

For information on these and other Lamar University Literary

Press books go to www.Lamar.edu/literarypress

Acknowledgments

Chip Dameron gratefully acknowledges the following publications in which some of these poems first appeared.

Amarillo Bay
Houston Chronicle
Langdon Review of the Arts in Texas
Narciso Martinez Cultural Arts Center Writers Forum Anthology
Ocotillo Review
San Antonio Express-News
San Pedro River Review
Texas Poetry Calendar
Weaving the Terrain: 100-Word Southwestern Poems

He also thanks Origami Poems Project for publishing the microchapbook, *At Paisano Ranch*, and appreciates the generous support he received from the Dobie Paisano Fellowship Program.

Betsy Joseph gratefully thanks the editors of *Texas Poetry Calendar 2017* for publishing one of the poems in her collection. This poem also appears in her collection *Only So Many Autumns* (Lamar University Literary Press) under the title "From My Mother's Voice."

CONTENTS

Betsy Joseph: *In Their Voices*

INTRODUCTION
by Carol Coffee Reposa

In pooling their talents to write this book, co-authors and siblings Chip Dameron and Betsy Dameron Joseph dip into an immeasurably creative tradition because family artistic collaborations probably have existed as long as have families themselves. It's not a stretch to imagine Paleolithic mothers and fathers, sisters and · brothers, working through the night to paint the walls of some dimly lit cave near Altamira or Lascaux with images designed to ensure a successful hunt, or performing a ritual chant to prepare for the undertaking. Many later examples of such partnerships come to mind too, including those of William and Dorothy Wordsworth, Robert and Clara Schumann, the Brontës, James Weldon and John Rosamond Johnson, and the Gershwins, not to mention Eddie Foy's boisterous family or the riotous Smothers Brothers. These of course represent only a miniscule sampling of the innumerable and often nameless family alliances that have helped to shape the trajectories of art, music, literature, and dance through the millennia. What sets *Relatively Speaking* apart is its seamless incorporation of current concerns and eternal mysteries, the timely and the timeless.

Texas Gumbo, Chip Dameron's portion of the collection, is aptly titled, as his taut, muscular lines survey life in the Lone Star State from the multiple perspectives of a Dobie Paisano Fellow, compassionate naturalist, aficionado of Texas highways and byways, and avid tennis player. He sees it all: the climate and geography of Texas, its sometimes tortured political history, that immensity of sea and sky, the checkered fortunes of the Rio Grande, above all the state's spectacularly varied flora and fauna. An entire section of *Texas Gumbo* examines meticulously the Rio Grande Valley's unique bird populations. No one who reads these poems is likely to forget his accounts of kiskadees, chachalacas, or crested caracaras that can "snare rabbits/...and tear out/ a calf's umbilical cord." Dameron recognizes the often porous boundaries of grace and danger, life and death. Of having to kill a gorgeous but poisonous snake that turns up on his back porch, he wonders "how many/ truths were packed into its vibrant beauty."

While some of his work muses on mortality and the relentless passage of time, he also finds abundant sources of hope and humor in the world he observes. In his eyes, pollinating Ashe junipers are "randy shagged/ evergreens,...// their rusty pollen/ detonating on time,...// a generous promise/ to every female tree." His delightful "Crisscrossing Texas, or 19 Ways of Looking at a Road Map" catalogues with precision and wit some of the state's memorably named towns:

> Woodworkers rejoice—there's fine lumber from Live Oak
> to Red Oak, White Oak to Lone Oak, Cottonwood
> to Mesquite, Magnolia to Pine Forest.

> You can follow the money from Dime Box to Dinero.

> Smart to pack some heat and an NRA sticker when visiting
> Gun Barrel City or Cut and Shoot.

His humor sometimes is laced with poignancy as in "First Set, Central Texas in August," which charts the efforts of "(f)our guys in their sixties and seventies" to put aside their "(c)ancer scares, knee and hip surgeries" and fill the morning with "crosscourt backhands, lobs, topspin forehands, some/ winners, some out." Age and physical limits notwithstanding, the men finish the set with "(f)ist pumps at net, congrats,/ friendly banter. Too many errors, but/ what the hell—every tennis day is good." Whether he's contemplating a star-spangled night in the Big Bend, considering the Buddhist implications of a chigger bite, or penning an offbeat tribute to Kinky Friedman, Chip Dameron brings to the poetic table a discerning eye and big heart, to the great good fortune of his readers.

The same may be said of his co-author and sister Betsy Joseph, but there the similarity ends, as the two employ decidedly different rhetorical strategies and structures. Joseph's contribution to the collection, *In Their Voices*, consists entirely of narrative monologues delivered by female personae, some speaking from the grave. These emotionally rich poems explore a broad range of topics, from agoraphobia and arranged marriage to Vietnam and the Great Depression, but all demonstrate the inextricable co-existence of hope and suffering, love and loss. Some of the speakers describe personal trials and triumphs like those of Cleva, who with grit and determination learns to fend for herself after the passing of a devoted husband. Others, though, confront such global events as JFK's assassination and the Holocaust. "Hannah's Story," for example, conveys unforgettably the anguish of a woman who continues to relive the ineradicable horror of internment in a Nazi concentration camp: "I still smell the stink and the illness.//... Ach, the guards are always coming for me./ Even when my son softly strokes my arm/ I see the uniforms behind him."

Some of these retrospective voices record startling transformations like that of Beverly, who morphs from an exotic dancer into a skilled auto mechanic. In the same vein, another woman, Irma, begins her career working in a dry goods store but ultimately serves as a high-level Federal agent: "It was then 1943./ I began my job in Intelligence and remained in D.C./ for the duration of the war./ And that is all I am going to say about that." Still other speakers review their near-misses and long shots, as in "Le Ha's Story," which traces the stages of her family's harrowing escape from Vietnam: "Boat 62. That was the number of the boat we took,/ and it turned out to be a good luck boat./ Many boats were fired on by North Vietnamese soldiers/...Some boats did not make it through storms/... Other boats were captured by pirates— ... But the captain of Boat 62 kept us safe."

Family life figures prominently in Joseph's work, recalling the famous opening sentence of Anna Karenina: "Happy families are all alike; every unhappy family is unhappy in its own way." Those speakers whose families are contented record and reflect the expected verities of goodwill, compassion, and harmony, but those who struggle at home narrate unpredictable mishaps and wrong turns. A case in point is Ethel, who ends up permanently estranged from her sister because of a misunderstanding about a recipe for pea salad. Another is Ruth, who against the odds manages to escape her murderous spouse: "I was told that statistically I shouldn't be alive./ Four hours of holding a gun to my head/ and knocking back cans of Schlitz,/ my husband's arm finally tired,/ and I got away." Contexts, motives, and outcomes vary widely in Joseph's domestic poems, but all attest the strength and intensity of familial bonds— for better or for worse.

While on a first reading the poems of Dameron and Joseph might seem wildly disparate, their respective visions ultimately intersect, especially when they address the redemptive power of love. Dameron sees such redemption in everyday miracles, "magical/ stuff of the quotidian" like an army of ants, "many sailing by/ with leaves thirty times their size" or the majesty of a live oak "older/ than the Republic." For Joseph, the deepest saving grace comes with enduring interpersonal love, love that transcends death, as epitomized in "My Mother Madgie's Story." In this haunting elegy, the speaker, now elderly and struggling with dementia, strives to be reunited with her late husband:

> I lived with a man for sixty-six years
> and one day he disappeared.
> At long last I decided to find him.
> I pulled at the air as if it were a veil,
> as if he were standing behind it
> in the gauze of pale light,
> in the lingering scent of lavender.

In such poems Chip Dameron and Betsy Dameron Joseph affirm not just their shared DNA but a profound spiritual kinship as well. Maybe that twelfth-century German proverb is right: "Blood is (indeed) thicker than water."

Texas Gumbo
Chip Dameron

At Paisano Ranch

House Bones

A two-room cabin
built in the 1860s,

hand-hewn cedar
logs and limestone

rock mortared into
a frontier infancy,

now grown along
with the rest of

Texas, expanded,
modernized, and

the uncovered bones
in the hallway are

but hints of what
the earth holds dear.

Creek

From the front porch,
Barton Creek's burbling

is the constant sound
all day long, until

the cicadas amp up.
Several feet deep

these days, flowing
on into Austin, it

was dry for two years
not so very long ago,

and then last spring it
flooded for six weeks.

I listen to its voice now,
tuned beyond meaning.

Coyote

I watch him glide
down the fence line,

early light crisping
his silvery brown coat,

and then another appears,
and two more, more

cautious, holding close
to safety, while the lead

coyote comes on across
the front yard, on

guard, not spotting me
through the window,

and after the others
ease toward the creek

he follows, satisfied
the coast is clear.

Grasses

A litany of grasses,
a song across
rocky meadows:

sideoats grama
plains lovegrass
blue grama

yellow Indiangrass
silver bluestem
Alamo switchgrass

little bluestem
Texas grama
big bluestem

sand dropseed
King Ranch bluestem
inland sea oats—

forage for cattle
and hungry minds.

Rampant Sex

Best to keep an eye
on the Ashe junipers,

those randy shagged
evergreens, thick

on the brushy hillside
and along the road,

their rusty pollen
detonating on time,

coating the valleys,
hills, neighborhoods,

a generous promise
to every female tree

of blue berries, seeds
to feed hungry birds

and coyotes, magical
stuff of the quotidian.

Grandfather Oak

I'll bet if Buddha
had been a Texan

he might have picked
this live oak, older

than the Republic,
have sat right under

the missing limb,
others reaching out

toward enlightenment.
What he might have

known as nirvana
through chigger bite

itching is a koan
ripe for meditation.

Down in the Valley

Still Life in Motion

This poem is yours, he says, as thousands
of ants scurry along their well-worn path

bordering the paved alley, many sailing by
with leaves thirty times their size, the line

stretching from their mound's entrance
to a pile of trimmings forty yards away,

and we both marvel at the procession
of seemingly tireless workers doing

what they're wired to do; our wiring
tells us to continue our Brownsville

ambling, our free-range musing, but before
we move on, I offer him the poem too.

Reflections

Late winter afternoon:
the resaca is spackled

with a galaxy of starbursts,
bending space like Einstein;

two orchids on the windowsill
flaunt knobby buds again;

then you gaze my way,
hedge against time's sorrows.

Red Touch Yellow

Refilled the feeder for tomorrow's green jays,
grackles, house sparrows, whistling ducks,

and there on the back porch by the door
a narrow gorgeously striped object, black

and yellow and red, moving slowly,
its bullet head stretching blackly upward

as it sought something in the dimming air.
Red touch yellow, kill a fellow, I remembered,

and thought about the two kids next door
and the border collie on the other side,

then got a shovel and severed the head.
When the body quit writhing, I pitched

both into the resaca at the foot of the yard,
sorry to have to take the snake's life,

and wondered as I turned back how many
truths were packed into its vibrant beauty.

Taking the Border's Temperature

I play tennis Sunday mornings
with a seasoned surgeon who lives

in Matamoros, a Mexican who
trained in Canada and England,

a painter of proven talent too,
who grafts skin for burn victims

and turns wealthy women's
faces into smoothened lies.

He listens for gunfire and
follows its echoes on Facebook.

He became an American
citizen this spring so he's got

an option if the Zetas infect
his hospital's vital arteries.

Back and forth across the bridge,
like a lively tennis match.

He's got the skills, knows which
shots to hit when, where

to move to make the right play
and win the game—for now.

South Texas Communion

While the Pope was touring D.C.
and shaking the nervous hands
of carefully chosen schoolchildren,
I watched a vermilion flycatcher
as it poised on a willow branch,
black masked but too orangy red
to pass for received doctrine,
and swallows zoomed around
on their mosquito orbits, quicker
than prayer, leaving it up to
the gaudy green jays in the oak tree
to talk about what it might mean
to behold the halo of light
after the afternoon's soft rain.

Rio Grande Valley Specialty Birds

Crested Caracara

It stands upright
by the road: dark body,
white neck, orange face,
regal in defiance,

waiting to resume
another bloody meal
some car provided
in the blinding night.

Quick on golden legs,
it can snare rabbits
too and tear out
a calf's umbilical cord.

Now it bends over
and shears off flesh
with its hooked beak,
blue as a soft spring sky.

Altamira Orioles

Inside that two-foot sock hanging
magically from a branch's end,
six fledglings squirm into air

and cry out for what they don't
have, eggs shattered and light
now the world they have

to live in, their fibrous nest
a mix of moss, epiphyte roots,
thin bark strips, palm fibers,

and stolen strands of yarn.
If they survive, orange and black
like Halloween spooks with

black daggered beaks, they'll
build new nests every year,
defying the laws of architecture.

Green Jay

Hard not to wonder how you
earned your gaudy coloration—

sky-blue head, black mask
and throat, back a blend

of emerald and blue, pale-green
belly, yellow tail coverts.

Still, somehow you disappear
into a live oak's leaves,

looking for the fattest acorns,
and between flights to cache

them you sound your raspy
shek shek shek shek, reminding

the world of your prominence,
bursting again into sunlight.

Aplomado Falcon

Years ago, strychnine killed off
the black-tailed prairie dogs

aplomado falcons preyed upon,
claws honed by a day's hunger,

poisoning many of them too, but
now I spot a juvenile on the refuge

road, a dove gripped for dinner,
cinnamon and gray mask the fatal

response to a perennial question,
and when it ascends, tail bars

ruddering the breeze, it defines
the old narrative's persistence

as it carries on the lonely, urgent
need it's been bequeathed.

Great Kiskadee

It bolts off a branch
to snag a flying insect,

aerial artistry worthy of
an act inside the big tent—

but peanuts compared
to mobbing a hawk

that threatens its nest,
driving the raptor off

and then returning to
the peacefulness of perch,

lemon breasted, rufous
winged, black masked,

watching for a fingerling's
glitter in the resaca below.

Black-Bellied Whistling Ducks

A cold north wind drives
February into everyone's bones.

Dropping out of a leaden sky,
whistling ducks invade the yard.

Ten rustle back and forth,
rooting for seeds under the feeder.

Two stand tall as sentinels,
one facing north, one south.

At whiskey hour they all pause,
alert, measuring the waning light.

Turn away a moment, turn back—
they've all disappeared.

Like a child you yearn to fly off
too, whistling into the dusk.

Chachalacas

In November, some hunters seek
chachalacas in tangled brush land,
roasting them for Thanksgiving.

Around town, drab-colored
and partridge-sized, they roost
in cedar elms and ebonies,

half successful in guarding
eggs against indigo snakes,
their raucous cackling chorus

CHA cha lac
CHA cha lac
CHA cha lac

waking the neighborhood
as light dances briskly
onto another day's stage.

Least Grebe

Smallest of the grebes,
with a golden button
of a burning eye,

it bobs and glides
and dives, bobs
and glides and dives,

the shallow muddy
water home to insects,
fish, whatever fattens.

As it moves on, I think
of Poe's pale blue eye,
clouded like a vulture's,

driving his mad storyteller
into a midnight rage
of unblinking blindness.

Olive Sparrows

At the refuge on the wrong
side of the border fence,

out-of-town birders slather
mosquito spray and binocular

thorny trees for migrating
warblers and flamboyant locals—

kiskadees, Altamira orioles,
green jays. Blending unseen

into native brush alongside
the trail, olive sparrows comb

leaf litter for insects and seeds,
oblivious to lists and egos.

Ringed Kingfisher

With a spiky crest that would
be coveted by any punk rocker,

the male ringed kingfisher waits
on a wire for a fishy miscue,

the dappled flicker all he needs
to launch a sonic strike,

ten-penny bill shattering
the morning calm, bird retreating

with his snared prize
to a stump, working it down

his gullet to the bottom
of his fine rufous belly,

blinking with satisfaction,
the light a mute accomplice.

South Texas Reverie

Early morning light
dappling the trees, a mug
of hot coffee in hand,
and the calls of mockingbirds
and doves crisscrossing the air.

Dawn Patrol, South Texas Coast

They emerge from the blue black
north sky in their squadrons,

six in a line or eleven or twenty
in a wavering vee, first light

from the sea giving them shape,
flap flap flap flap flap glide,

brown spans, yellow-daggered beaks,
the leader looking for silver

in the unfurling surf, past
the jetties and armed olive green

men stationed at the mouth
of the once-great river, then

they angle down and skim
the faces of Mexican waves,

disappearing into the ambiguities
of another day's sunlit distance.

End of the Rio Grande

We parked at the end of the road,
last stop in South Texas, and walked
an hour in the early light, the sea
a bountiful blue, the brown pelicans
patrolling overhead, the day promising
clean heat and clear lines of sight.

Ahead, a lone green and white van
marked one side of the river, or so
it seemed, the white sand it guarded
no different than the sand a yard
farther on. We could just make out,
a hundred yards to the west, the last
glint of the drought-deadened river.

Standing in the parched river bed
were a man on this side, a woman
and a baby on the other, their words
muffled by the laughing gulls' cries,
another border story, another dry day,
the waves rolling in, rolling in.

Listen Closely

Does the blue-green sea ever stop
calling out our birth names?

The mockingbird hears us talking
and talking, and at sundown
it tells us *go home, go home.*

The Gulf never stops naming us,
one by one, as we disappear.

Around the State

Crisscrossing Texas, or 19 Ways of Looking at a Road Map

Bee Cave to Honey Grove, Big Lake to Little River,
Sweetwater to Sour Lake, Kingsville to Queen City,
Newgulf to Old Ocean—lots of towns with ties.

You can breakfast in Early, lunch at Noonday,
and hustle west to Sundown for dinner.

Caution light in the Panhandle: avoid an endless
yo-yo between Loop and Circle Back.

Artists, load up your palettes with rich hues
from Amarillo, Orange, Black, Blanco, and Silver,
plus side stops in Blue Ridge, Brownwood, Red Rock,
and Goldsboro.

History buffs might opt to zigzag through twenty-three
presidential towns, including Washington and Jefferson,
Lincoln and Roosevelt, Reagan and Johnson City.

Woodworkers rejoice—there's fine lumber from Live Oak
to Red Oak, White Oak to Lone Oak, Cottonwood
to Mesquite, Magnolia to Pine Forest.

You can follow the money from Dime Box to Dinero.

Smart to pack some heat and an NRA sticker when visiting
Gun Barrel City and Cut and Shoot.

Martyrs can follow Crockett and Bowie to Fate and Alamo.

Relive the Battle of San Jacinto by starting with Houston
and going all the way to Santa Anna.

To track appropriated tribes, strike out from Seminole and drive
east and north to Cherokee, Comanche, Caddo, and Tioga.

Looking for wildlife? Go first to Buffalo, then White Deer,
and on to Turkey.

Lovers should take Rising Star to Venus, then spend
a dreamy day in Valentine.

Pilgrims can pray in Palestine and Nazareth, contemplate
Corpus Christi, and be renewed in Trinity.

How to choose between Eden and Paradise? Try them both,
with detours in Godley and Devine.

If you have the travel itch, hopscotch from Holland to China,
Scotland to Iraan, Paris to Roma to Athens to Moscow.

In March, stop in Shamrock to get your green on the way
to the big parade in Dublin.

When you're driving from Electra to Pandora, watch out
for complexes and boxes.

And if Shakespeare were alive and traveling from Stratford
to London, he could pause on the way and try to revive
poor Desdemona.

Six Flags over Texas

It's a strange six-pointed state—
frying pan handle holding
down the great plains northward,
gun grip keeping frontier order
in the far west, saw-toothed
sickle securing the south,
cypress river bounding the east.

The land has been shaped
by its waves of dominion—
today's stars and stripes,
interpolated by the ill-fated
stars and bars, proudly preceded
by the lone star, which supplanted
the ongoing fight between eagle
and serpent; farther back,
the floating golden fleurs-de-lis,
and earliest of the colonial
claims, the crowned rojigualda.

Native peoples needed no colored
cloth to mark their territories,
fighting or coexisting by creek,
limestone hill, or pine forest—
Comanche and Apache, Caddo,
Tonkawa, Coahuiltecan,
Karankawa. Today some have
official flags, as if these can tell
what it meant to be part of this
brazen disjointed landscape,
long before the rest of us arrived,
long before they lost their last
battle and turned into ghosts.

Texas History Lesson

Fine driving south in April, scissortails
on telephone wires, bright coral swaths
of Indian paintbrush along the roadside,
mesquites boasting their chartreuse vigor.
Nixon comes and goes quickly, one mile
square of pickups beside modest homes
and Mustang Stadium, big enough
to hold all 2,200 on football Fridays.

Some 17 miles farther south, halfway
to Kenedy, new caliche roads lead
to dozens of fracking operations—
fat cylindrical storage tanks, skinny
towers flaring burn-off gases, salt-water
disposal wells threatening the groundwater.
While specialized tanker rigs rumble by,
Disinterested cows graze the fields.

Kenedy has more bustle, though many
shops along its three-block downtown
are shuttered; the action's on Highway 181.
The town holds a bluebonnet festival
each spring—I missed it—and was called,
a hundred years ago, "six-shooter junction."
Nixon has its two Ns, but Kenedy is short
one, named for Mifflin and not John F.

Still, hard not to contemplate obvious
contrasts and think hero and villain,
martyr and crook, yet such labels never
tell the whole story, for both have the blood
of 50,000 soldiers on their headstones
(as does LBJ, buried west in Johnson City),
separated by the breadth of a continent,
evoked by two obscure Texas neighbors.

McCamey
in Grandad's voice

We pulled up stakes in Sherwood
and drove the Model T west
to the dusty oil boom in Texon,
then on in '26 to the new well
further west, tents mushrooming
by the week next to the nearby
railroad siding, ten thousand of us
by the next year. Annie and me
opened up the first restaurant, which
durn near killed us, oil workers
and fancy ladies coming in all
day and night, driving us to build
and run a boarding house instead.
Good living till the big crash
took the town's refinery with it.
Life shrank, then limped along.
And George McCamey, who drilled
the well with Gilbert Johnson?
His name stuck when the tents
became a town, but he never lived
here, stopping by from time to time,
too busy wildcatting elsewhere
or enjoying the genteel fineries
of Fort Worth. His thumbprint's
still here, though, and the new
derricks now harvest only the wind
that blows day and night against
the letters on my gravestone.

[In 2001 the Texas legislature named McCamey
"the Wind Energy Capital of Texas."]

Bending Springtime

Four pals, we stayed three nights in Marathon.
Not *that* Marathon, the immortalized
Greek plain, but the humble Texas hamlet
doubling as one gateway to Big Bend's park:
high desert and mountains, river and rock,
where we hiked to the Window until heat
drove us hobbling back to Chisos Basin,
then the long loop to the red-cliffed canyon,
Santa Elena, left side belonging to Mexico
and right the U.S., the half-dry Rio Grande
winding tamely through its gouged ancestry.
Humbled ourselves, we took the unpaved road
out, every thirteen-mile jolt and shudder,
joked about buying one of the mesas
north of Terlingua, then dined in Alpine.

Next day we toured Fort Davis: county seat,
historic fort, mountain range as backdrop,
our plan to join the observatory
star party later, but the clouds thickened
and we wended our way back to our house,
binge watched a British dramedy series,
and turned in at midnight. Mike woke at five,
stepped out into a dark sky's dream, and roused
us up and outside, where the Milky Way
spangled the night's skin like a sailor's map,
shooting stars zoomed across and flamed out,
and satellites followed their preordained paths,
while a thunderstorm on the north skyline
presaged the coming light of a new day.
When we left, time took us onward once again.

Name Dropping

In Austin they pulled Jeff Davis's statue off
its pedestal, the slave proponent and Confederate

leader (or traitor) then restored to his bronze
origin and contextualized in a campus museum.

What to make of what's way out west:
2,258 square miles of county, mountains,

town, fort, and state park, named for the man
who was Secretary of War under Pierce

before embodying the bloody consequences
of secession. To us, place names matter.

But to the volcanic rocks of the region,
to the cacti and junipers, mountain lions

and pronghorn antelope, dark turns to light
and back to dark, utterly nameless.

Dog Days

Dawn glides in on a breeze.
Titmice flit from tree to feeder.
A spiny lizard tours its territory.

Deer cross the field, foraging.
Heat builds, expands, engulfs.
Native grasses teem with chiggers.

The sun blisters the sky's blue.
Whatever moves seeks shade.
Plants lick light, draw inward.

Cicadas fill the humid air
with their static symphony.
The west bakes a sunset.

Light finally leaches away.
Dusk takes the day to dark.
Titmice, lizard, deer become dreams.

First Set, Central Texas in August

Four guys in their sixties and seventies
spin for partners, take the court, warm up,
game on. They're out before the heat
turns legs to rubber, willpower to a whisper.

Cancer scares, knee and hip surgeries,
be damned. Slicing serves, crosscourt
backhands, lobs, topspin forehands, some
winners, some out. Grumbles and chuckles.

One-love. Then two. An ace, couple
of forehands into the net, a backhand long.
Down three-love. Switch sides, drink water.
Waggish trash talk back and forth.

Overhead down the line, dying drop shot,
on and on to ad and deuce and ad,
then winner drilled deep up the middle,
as accurate as Federer could drive it.

Three-one. Then three-two. More water,
a minute sitting in the windscreen's shade,
back to the battle. Lots of quick surges,
defensive returns, clean put aways.

Still, the lead grows: four-two, five-two,
then six-two. Fist bumps at net, congrats,
friendly banter. Too many errors, but
what the hell—every tennis day is good.

May Day

Texas heat wears down
gray foxes too—
this one glides between
wrought-iron bars,

heads for the birdbath,
up on hind legs,
chin scraping the lip,
laps up cool water.

It paces a bit
on the river stones
and then arcs through
the fence, jogging

across prairie grass,
melting into scrub brush,
absent from the sun's
overexposed snapshot.

Hill Country Snow Dust

Overnight, birdsong
and the tang of air turned white—
who needs color now?

Christmas Tree Rings

A cold sunny new year's start
in Dallas: we'd split up and scoured
the alleys, snagging pines and firs,
still tinseled or flocked white or pink,
dragging them into our backyards,
fashioning forts to be defended:
bloodthirsty yells, rapid attacks,
wrestling for life on the dead grass.
When darkness drove us inside,
our mothers fixed mugs of cocoa
and listened to us chatter on
about our cooked-up conquests.
With green and ever rising sap,
we never imagined our roots
would be severed, the alleys closed,
the forts invaded by strangers.

Solitary Caw

Now that the world has again
turned the green of money,
of envy, of those long days

long ago when time turned
slower than it ever will
today and every tomorrow,

something springs eternal,
not hope exactly, that bird
with fine iridescent feathers

you see when light pushes
darkness into another time
zone, but a desire to absorb

what is refracted in the caw
of the crow crossing the field
nearby, that solitary caw.

Nightfall

The mesquite's main trunk bends up
to the waist and then stretches

into the twilight's thinnest blue,
Medusa-headed, arms open to small

birds and celebrating rootedness
in air, offering a speechless dancer's

answer to the rising darkness,
extinguishing what can be seen

but not the texture of what
has been felt, what comes back

in dreams, and behind the murkiness
you sense something is moving,

ready to step out into moonlight,
take your hand, spin you around,

and send you bounding across
the yard, leaping out of your life.

Habitation

The deed says I own this stone house,
nestled in a neighborhood of stone houses,
along with the garden by the back fence,
the bur oaks, Shumard red oaks, cedar elms,
crepe myrtles; it's my lot to give them water
through the blistering Texas summers,
tend to trimming and raking, thankful
a younger man mows and edges the grass.

I have no hold on the resident squirrels
and visiting gray fox, nor on the doves
and titmice and robins and cardinals
that freely share the trees, garden, yard.

I guess the mineral rights are mine,
a quarter acre's worth, but I've found
no clause covering the clouds above
or the breeze that rattles the leaves.
Still, I'm satisfied enough, knowing
that deeds are nothing more than paper;
there's a perpetual joke in play, where
I'm the squatter in the cosmic punch line.

Tex Mex Lingo

Hill Country ranchers turned Pedernales
into a truncated Perd-nal-es,

Austin folks say Man-shack
whenever they see Manchaca,

Santa Anna lost twice when San Jacinto
became Texanized as San Juh-sin-to,

and best not to ask about Guadalupe,
Refugio, Bolivar, Llano, or Palacios,

or grieve for a tilde when nachos
come loaded with chopped ha-la-pee-nos.

Kinky Times in Granbury

Maybe the best way to wrap up
a four-day festival of writers
and artists in Texas is to get
real kinky with the real Kinky,
that original Texas Jewboy,
decked out in his signature getup,
black hat, cowboy boots, unlit cigar.

The man who nearly became governor—
"I won every state except Texas"—
moves skillfully from song to joke
to song again, his voice now gruff,
now melodious, sipping as needed
his 80 proof "Mexican mouthwash"
to clarify where he's going next.

After romping through that iconic
tweak of feminism (biscuits in oven,
buns in bed), he's on to the mystical
in his latest CD, "Resurrected,"
bringing to life a panhandling
savior at Denny's: "Jesus in Pajamas."
And last, a tribute story for his father.

So sixty listeners clap, the Jewboy winks;
the show is over—they're now unkinked.

In Their Voices
Betsy Joseph

Encounters

Elsa's Story

It is not that my life is cloaked in mystery.
I just don't care to divulge all the details.
A snippet here and there, but the whole of it?
No, it stays with me.

I did share some snippets once—
and even my name—
in a nail salon of all places.
It's curious what one will mention to a stranger
sitting across the same narrow table
while our nails are drying under the heat lamp.

The conversation began with a comment on my accent—
innocuous, certainly, but it startled me all the same.
The younger woman just seemed to be exchanging pleasantries.
It is, after all, rather awkward to ignore one
sitting directly across from you.

Still I revealed only a scant amount of information:
that I spent my childhood in Berlin,
that I lived in a privileged neighborhood,
that my father, so gallant in his officer's uniform,
moved our family far from relatives to South America
after Germany was defeated . . .

My encounter with Elsa and her story planted a seed for a project that took over twenty years to germinate. I was fairly confident about the way her story would have fleshed out had she continued with it. She did not elaborate further, however, perhaps sensing my curiosity might have prompted further questions she did not want to encourage.

This woman shared what was certainly a compelling story which gave rise to speculations, considering the time and history of her youth—speculations that left me wanting the rest of the story, the *whole* story.

Following that chance occurrence, I began to listen more closely to other women's stories. I found many of them fascinating, meaningful, and often quite surprising. I listened intently to details so that I could recreate the experiences shared with me.

With this collection I am a poet-storyteller. The stories and the voices, though, belong to an array of women in the pages that follow. I have been the privileged audience to these individuals' accounts of challenges, adversities, acceptance, disappointment, confusion, and even fear. And with a number of these amazing women, I became witness to their ultimate triumphs.

I hope I have done justice to them all.

Myra's Story: The Man Who Loved to Fly

In Barrow, Alaska stands a monument to two men:
an aviator and a well known humorist.
Both made unwise decisions resulting in bad luck—
namely their deaths on August 15, 1935.

Some folks are determined to see a dream come true.
That was Will Rogers.
Like other dreamers, he relied on the funding
of successful businessmen, such as my uncle, Wiley Post.

Their air voyage to Alaska was ill-fated from the start,
these friends flying a plane not only constructed
from the remains of two others
but also too heavy in the nose.

Some dreams die hard
and the dreamers and adventurers die with them.

In my eighties now,
I have never made the journey to Barrow,
though other family members have traveled there.

It is unlikely I ever will.
In my mind, though, I still picture
the uncle my eight-year-old self adored—
a man who more than anything loved to fly.

Cotton's Story: New Words

The Great Depression
was a tough time for a good many folks,
my family included.
When my mother died after the last baby was born,
my daddy held us together as long as he could.
There wasn't enough food much of the time,
but we stayed busy playing and looking after one another.
My brothers and sisters all called me "Cotton"
because I was such a towhead.
I'm still called Cotton today.

My oldest brother married at sixteen,
my oldest sister at fifteen.
For my daddy that meant two less mouths to feed.
Another brother and sister were later taken in
by an aunt and uncle—another two less to feed.
That just left me and my little brother.

When I was nine and my brother was six,
Daddy took us for a drive in the old truck.
We finally stopped in front of a big white house—
the largest I had ever seen—
with four big pillars from the porch to the roof.
Daddy rapped on the door a couple of times
until a lady wearing her Sunday-best answered.

She didn't seem surprised to see three strangers on her porch,
and she was smiling kindly at my brother and me.
Daddy had taken off his hat and swept it along his side
as if trying to dust off his coveralls.

The still smiling lady opened the door more widely
as my daddy knelt beside us.

"I can't care for you good enough anymore," he rasped.
"You both will stay at this nice house from here on."
He awkwardly hugged us as we stood bewildered
and then he hurriedly walked back to the truck.

He never glanced back
and I saw him only one other time in my life.

I learned a new word that day: *orphanage.*
I remained there 'til I graduated from high school
and married James, a boy who also grew up there.

I learned another word many years later
while taking a class on writing life memories.
The word was *cathartic.*
It means a purging or cleansing.
The instructor wrote it on a white board
and told us that this kind of writing
helps us to free ourselves.

I came to love the word
and liked the way it rolled off my tongue
and into my writing.
I also liked to flaunt the word from time to time
in Bible class and at bridge club.

But my vanity is not my point.
I never thought I could tell this story
without stirring up raw feelings.
But I've done it now and feel a whole lot better
getting this load of longtime hurt off my heart.
It's been cathartic.

Hannah's Story: The Camp

I am only dimly aware of present time.
I know I live in a place where I did not raise my children.
I know I spend my time in a wheelchair.
I know my son visits on Shabbat
and recites the Kiddush prayer.
I think I even sing in Hebrew with him.

I was fourteen when my family was taken.
Lately the camp seems more real than this place where I now live.
I still smell the stink and the illness.
I still await the news or sight of mother or father
even as I sit in this dining hall among strangers with blank faces.

It seems I have frequent outbursts of shouting and crying.
I hear myself in Polish screaming, "Don't let the guards take me!"
Kind people soothe and restrain me, my ears hear their gibberish,
but still I see the guards behind them.

The guards are always coming for me,
even when Benny Goodman is playing his clarinet.
Ach, the guards are always coming for me.
Even when my son softly strokes my arm
I see the uniforms behind him.

Ruthie's Story: We Do What We Do

I was a wartime bride
early in the Vietnam War.
I met my husband in San Diego,
married him after a whirlwind romance.
He then shipped out and I stayed behind.

It was what war brides did.

He did return, more quiet than before he left,
and we did what was expected:
settled down, raised a family,
and became full-fledged adults.
Easier for me than for my husband
who lost interest in a successful career
and decided to become a farmer.

The move from California to Missouri
filled him with excitement and me with doubt.
His trading an office at E.F. Hutton for a barn with two lofts
was not a change I had bargained for.
Not everyone realizes the Sixties were not all Hippie-Dippie;
those of us who married early in that decade
still tended to follow general traditions, such as
a wife following her husband in his pursuits.

It is just what we did.

Now I am almost seventy-six.
I lost my husband to ALS
after caring for him nearly six years.
It was a tough time for both of us,
but we were together to his end.

Now I travel the country all on my own.
I have driven to each coast,
even venturing into Canada.
Asked if I am ever afraid, I always shake my head "No."
I am content that my last destination will be death.
Until that time
I hope to cover much more ground and make friends of strangers.

Linh's Story: Only One Great Love

I gaze at my reflection in the water
and see an elder staring back:
deep-set eyes with many lines etched like the sun's rays,
iron hair pulled back in a loose coil,
my eighty-something years of skin
hanging loose and uneven.

My mind, though, is sharp and can slice
through memories like a knife
shaving a mud carp, with ease and grace.
I have lived long in the province of Tra Vinh
and fished in the Mekong River, polluted now.
My memories run deep, like the river bottom.

In my time boys and girls did not attend the same school,
but we all gathered for events and celebrations.
During upper school two boys liked me.
It did not seem to matter they were best friends,
but when they both pronounced love for me, I had to choose.
Bao, slender and studious, was gently protective
and his quiet presence calmed me.
Duong was Bao's opposite: physically strong and confident.
He liked to run in a circle around me to make me dizzy and laugh.

I was then young but knew I would not always be,
so I responded to the strong voice in my head,
allowing flattery's flutter to ease from my heart.
I chose Bao.

We worked as partners in the life we formed together,
created a home and a beautiful family.
Duong found a girl who liked to get dizzy and laugh,
and I believe they made a good life, too.

Sixty-four years together Bao and I shared
before his body tired and illness shrank
the skin from his bones.
Finally his heart's beating ceased.
Duong had lost his wife a few years earlier
and came to honor his best friend's death.

Soon he became a frequent traveler to my house,
still confident, still able to make my mouth
stretch into a smile even in my grief.

After a suitable length of time
Duong asked to share our last years together.
With a back stooped by age, his hands deeply veined,
his voice was strong, his words were soft.
But I was not tempted to take a second husband,
even one as dear as this old familiar friend.

All those years ago my head had chosen Bao.
I had chosen a lake with few ripples.
And then my heart had followed with gladness.
My memories are still enough for me as I wait out my time.
I feel Bao still by my side, still protecting me quietly.

Cleva's Story: No Shame in a Good Cry

Now that I am a widow
I realize just how much Harold took care of us,
how he handled matters so I would not have to worry.
I thought I was independent when I went to work
after our children grew up and left.
I was out in the world, it was true,
but Harold was still making sure our lives ran smoothly.

When he passed away—far too soon for me—
I learned to cook for one, to sleep alone,
and to locate a reliable handyman.
As long as there were no hitches, I managed fairly well.
Then came the afternoon when I lost my new grounding.

I returned from the grocery store to discover several things:
my garage door would not open, the gate to the back door
was padlocked—from the other side of the fence—
and my front door was latched on the inside.
I sat in my car wondering what Harold would do
until I realized this would not have happened to him.
Harold never got into pickles like this.

Did I mention this happened on a hot July afternoon?
My groceries were melting, my frustration was building,
and still I sat in the car with all the windows down
wondering what Harold would have me do.

Feeling helpless and foolish, I began to cry.
I don't think I cried this hard and long
since the doctor pronounced Harold dead that harsh May morning.
For a moment I wondered what neighbors might think.
Then I suddenly decided that there is no shame in a good cry,
so I allowed myself a noisy one, so noisy apparently
that some of the dogs along the alley joined in with me.

It was time to square my shoulders.
I opened the car door, grabbed my purse and keys,
gave the fence a serious look-over, and proceeded to climb.
There were some tricky moments during the hoisting and lowering,
but I made it to the ground intact without snagging my slacks.
Finally entering my air-conditioned home, I never gave another thought
about what Harold might have said or done.

Instead I was thinking how proud I was to figure it out on my own, and not finding a bit of shame in a good cry.

London's Story: My Normal Life

I have had many names as an adult,
have had to change them frequently
in order to protect myself.
I savor each name I choose,
let it roll first in my head and then on my tongue
until it feels right.

Ten years ago I needed a new name
and I wanted to try on "Paris,"
but that skinny blond model had made the name international.
Crossed that one off my list.
I chose "London" instead.
Second best, but it still sounded cosmopolitan
and the people looking for me would be thrown off,
expecting "Barbara," "Katherine," or perhaps "Marlene."
Imagine: Me sporting the "chin up" confidence
of the capital city of England!

Each name change has ushered in a new identity
with an adrenaline rush that often makes me talk nonstop,
my ringed hands a flurry of motion.

I daresay fellow students think me strange,
this near middle-aged woman in their midst
checking everything out while appearing self-possessed.
If they only knew I was the target of a sinister group,
they would certainly feel less significant.
They definitely couldn't manage a normal life
as I have these past twenty years.

I realize this game of cat and mouse, of hide and seek
cannot go on forever.
At some point I will become careless,
my artful dodging no longer successful.
Someone will find me.
I have grown weary of changing destinations,
of sustaining friendships that prove short term.
And each time I move I have to find a new therapist
who, like the previous ones, just prescribes a regimen of medication.

Ethel's Story: Blood and Trust

You would think you would know your own sister.
Not just because you grew up playing with one another,
but because you also later lived next door
to each other for twenty-five years.
It never occurred to me that Stella would ever doubt my word,
but she did.
And it resulted in twenty years of silence.
All because of a recipe.
Who would have thought it?

Stella was a good cook but considered me a better one.
Which is why she wanted my recipe for pea salad
for an important church potluck supper.
I offered to make it for her, but she insisted
that then it wouldn't be hers—
which it wasn't anyway, but I let that be.

She took the recipe over the phone while I patiently dictated
all the ingredients and their assembly.
That was the last friendly conversation we had.

The morning following the potluck Stella rang my front bell.
Normally she would have come around back,
so I should have known something wasn't quite right.
But I was washing up the breakfast dishes, my mind elsewhere.
The fury in Stella's voice let me know straight away
that this was no social call.
And her refusal to come inside meant I had to step out on the porch
where she accused me of sabotaging her pea salad.
No amount of listening and explaining could convince her otherwise.

She truly believed I had changed my own recipe
just to humiliate her before the whole church.
I told her I never would, my voice matching the volume of hers.
I even suggested going over the recipe again to prove my good will.
But it was too late.
Stella believed I had wronged her.

I hoped that in time she would come around, come to her senses,
and we would maybe get a laugh out of it.
But she couldn't seem to shake it and let it go.
I sure missed Stella's company and her voice

and when we would see each other out front at times,
she purposely looking away from me,
a great sadness would fill me.

I don't know if my sister came to my funeral when I died.
Blood may be thicker than water—
at least that's what people say—
but when it came to trust,
it seemed to make no difference in this case.

Judy's Story: Advice to a Roommate

I was the lackadaisical roommate,
probably more talented with charcoal and watercolor
than I knew or cared, but certainly lacking in true ambition.
I divided much of my time between
working at Burger King and smoking pot with my boyfriend.
Later I referred to that period as *my less productive years.*
My college roommate, on the other hand,
had a rhythm and purpose quite different from my own.
By that I mean she tended to wake up for classes
while I tended to sleep in.
Despite our different approaches to learning and cleaning,
we got along surprisingly well.

Sometimes I would caution that she was *too* dependable,
too predictable, and she would roll her eyes
while heading to the library after dinner, *predictably.*

One birthday I gave her a card
with a bird clearly upside down on the front.
Inside I had written, "Try flying upside down.
It's more unpredictable."
She rolled her eyes at me but smiled.

Though cancer took me away at age thirty-two,
she and I managed some visits before that happened.
We exchanged tidbits about the past and the present,
I confessing to finding my way finally,
she admitting to some free-form flip maneuvers—
though with precarious results at times.

The day before my life ended
she shared cinnamon toast and weak tea with me,
playfully transferred her headband to my bald head
before rushing off, *responsibly,* to pick her sons up from school.
A better parting gift was knowing she'd taken a roommate's advice,
and I told her so as I watched her leave for the last time.

Charlotte's Story: Double Life

I might as well have been in espionage,
I became so adept at living a double life.
I had two primary selves, you see:
My role as wife and then mother, as well as
my vocation as pediatric nurse
(and the sometimes fourth at a bridge table).
I learned to switch fluidly between the two halves,
but I never confused them.
Oh no, I never confused them.

Let me explain.
At home I was never pretty, bright, sexy, or witty enough.
I know this because my husband's reminders
became a dull echo in my heart.
I endeavored to be more,
but as far as my husband was concerned,
I didn't deliver. Was I even adequate?
I didn't dare ask.

In my other life I prospered, even exceeded expectations.
I knew that was the real me, but I could not bring her home.

When each turned eighteen, my children escaped,
left home to discover brighter vistas, develop healthier norms.
I was glad for them.
Unlike their mother, they had the excuse to launch themselves.

No one would have understood if I had left.
I had made a "good marriage."
My husband was quite successful in his career,
and he knew how to behave well in public.
We did, in fact, make a handsome couple.
I've no doubt my friends envied all that I possessed,
based on what they saw.
Clearly I had been clever in my cover-ups.
It was a bitter irony then.
It remains a bitter irony now.

In the end my husband's liver could not handle
all the bourbon freely sipped at the various galas,
soirées, the country club gatherings.
When he died people might have wondered

how I would manage, how I could live
without his strength that had presided over our marriage.

That strength almost crushed me.

But the advantage of a double life is that other life I led—
the one that valued me, acknowledged my contributions,
the one that kept me half whole.

Sarah's Story: Familiar Strangers

I was in my early sixties
when my memory began to fail me.
My husband and sons teased me at first,
thinking I had too many distractions
and couldn't keep things straight.

The distractions either increased
or my ability to recollect worsened with time.
No one wanted to address it, so I did.
I consulted a doctor, endured the battery of tests.

The diagnosis was early onset dementia.
The prognosis was not pretty.
The disease was accelerating rapidly.
I required more care, could not remain at home,
so we found a lovely facility that would see me
all the way through to the end.

When I began seeing strangers in the once familiar faces
all around me, I felt lost.
My world continued to narrow.
I could look at pictures in magazines,
but I could no longer read the words
within the many books inside my room.

Then my speaking became babbling,
which sounded frightening even to my ears.
We don't quite forget *everything*, as it turns out.
We can still tell when things are missing.

A man comes almost every day to see me.
He is gentle and kind and sometimes his voice
jumpstarts a memory in my mind.
He feeds me popcorn from a bowl,
placing a puffed kernel on my tongue.
And because I can no longer remember what to do,
I hear him say, "Chew, Sarah, chew.
Now swallow."
Over and over again.

Le Ha's Story: Crossing the Border

Many Vietnamese immigrants have their own boat story.
This is mine.

Even after the American War—
after all the Americans left—
the government in the north declared victory,
beginning the march south to make communists
of us all. Saigon fell first.
Then provinces like ours, Can Tho, came next.
Worried about our family, my husband
and so many others began making plans.
Crossing the border plans.
Escaping became our only hope.
We finally left in 1981, our family of four
and me eight months pregnant with our third child.

Boat 62. That was the number of the boat we took,
and it turned out to be a good luck boat.
Many boats were fired on by North Vietnamese soldiers
while still on the Mekong River.
Some boats did not make it through storms,
and every person on board drowned.
Other boats were captured by pirates—
terrible animals who robbed men of their money,
women of their jewelry, and who took young girls captive.
But the captain of Boat 62 kept us safe.

During the five days we traveled to Malaysia,
I was seasick for the first three,
not able to keep down the only food we had—
a small amount of rice and water for each of us.
I was getting scared for my baby.
On the fourth day the boat owner's wife came to me
with a cup of Ovaltine mixed with condensed milk.
I was not sick again.
She prepared a cup of this mixture three more times
before we landed at the camp in Malaysia.
We had become refugees, Vietnam far behind us.

When my pains came on, I was not afraid.
Birthing my first two children had been easy,
so it didn't worry me there was no doctor in our camp.

My baby boy was born very healthy in this different country.
More good luck.
And the luck followed us when we left Malaysia on the same boat
three long months later, now a family of five,
going to San Francisco to be safe in the U.S. at last.

Not long ago the thought came to me
that I have lived in America for thirty-nine years—
more years than I lived in my homeland.
In my heart I will always be Vietnamese,
but I have great love for this country, too.

Right now I know many Americans are angry
about so many things:
the pandemic, the protests, the politics.
Yes, these are hard times,
and I feel ups and downs, too,
but I crossed the border of my homeland
almost forty years ago for a better life.
My heart reminds me every day that America
opened its border to my family and gave us
the chance for better work, better chances for our children.

Some things may be wiser to forget,
but I never want to forget to be grateful.

Connie's Story: Who I Am

If you asked me to describe myself,
I would proudly proclaim that I am Black, large, and triumphant.
I am a woman of faith so unwavering
that I embrace my reading disability,
seeing it not as a weakness but as an obstacle I can overcome.

I am a middle-aged woman
who sashays through college corridors
relishing that they are gateways to further learning.

And oh do I want to learn—
even though my eyes scramble letters and my mind
can't put them in their right places
so that my mouth can catch up.

I am big, Black, and unmarried,
but I dress in bright colors and wear bold jewelry
so that people who see and consider me,
these people will look beyond my color,
my size, my age, my gender, and my disability.

I will not need to raise my voice to be heard.
My whisper will be loud enough to announce me
as I stand on the stage of becoming.

Sometimes in the mirror of my mind
I see myself as an ordinary version of Oprah Winfrey—
Yes, I do—
my dyslexia overshadowed by my grit.

Beverly's Story: The World's a Stage

People from my past commonly raise their eyebrows
when they learn that I ultimately became an auto mechanic.
They try to fathom my transition from exotic dancer to grease monkey,
and the leap is often too great for them to make.
I get it.

As a single mother of two young boys,
I didn't find many avenues open to someone with a GED
and limited job experience that would pay the bills—
with my clothes on.
While I'm not proud of putting my body on display,
receiving validation in the form of cat-calls—and worse,
I am proud that I wasn't on welfare and raising my sons
in Section Eight housing, exposing them to druggies—and worse.

But my sons were getting older and becoming wiser.
They thought I was bartending at a club in the evenings
when I left them with a sitter.
By day I was working on a college degree, which made them proud,
but I knew it was only a matter of time before they figured out
how I really made a living for the three of us.

Because my home life growing up was less than stable,
I spent afternoons after school and long summer days
at my grandfather's gas station.
He let me clean people's windshields and eventually pump gas,
but my favorite pastime was watching him work on cars.
I paid attention and asked questions and he turned out to be
the best teacher during my unsettled life.

After my sons started school, I decided to start college.
I did well in my classes. I loved the environment,
but I couldn't find my passion and purpose
until the day I wandered into the automotive tech building.
And then I knew.

I enrolled in a certificate program, received a scholarship
that allowed me to leave my night job, and I was on my way.
Instead of a skimpy costume, I proudly wore a work shirt and pants.
And above my shirt pocket, my name stitched in cursive.

Upon my completion, Toyota hired me right out of the gate. All I recall of graduation is the whooping of two young males as I walked across the stage—a stage I was proud to cross— such a far cry from the stage that once demeaned me.

Bobbie's Story: Chrysalis to Butterfly

My life has been a history of avoidances.
I will detour several blocks, taking extra minutes,
just to avoid turning left at a busy intersection.
I have turned down jobs if a building has more than six floors,
for I am terrified of elevators and must use the stairs.

For some years I would only leave the house
to take my daughter to and from school.
I never attended her events,
and my husband did the grocery shopping.

I did not know the word "agoraphobic"
until I read a magazine article that listed the signs.
I learned I was one of those people.
I also discovered that I was not a lost cause.

Slowly—very slowly—I emerged from my sheltered state.
Finally I was even able to register for college classes.
Imagine that.
I became a college student at the age of fifty.

I would be lying if I said I am completely cured.
I still avoid left turns at intersections,
and people behind me should be glad that I do.
I've also been known to hyperventilate
when I must take an elevator.
Old habits die hard, I guess.
Still, I've come a long way, baby.

Susan's Story: My Father's Decision

I was ten when President John F. Kennedy was assassinated.
Ten and living in Fort Worth where the reported assassin,
Lee Harvey Oswald, had also lived while growing up.
Ten and living with my family, the head of which was my father,
then executive director of the Fort Worth Council of Churches.

We were an ordinary family until we were not.
And like most Americans, we were glued to the TV all weekend,
first digesting the assassination, then Oswald's arrest,
followed two days later by his death at the hands of Jack Ruby.
After Oswald was shot, the air in our house seemed to shift.
My father was spending less time in front of the television
and more time on the phone in earnest yet subdued conversation.

My brother and I didn't yet know our father was desperately trying
to line up a pastor to preside over Oswald's funeral.
It became complicated when no one volunteered for the task.
After all, who would want that job?
But my father persisted in his search, finally locating a brave soul.

The day of Oswald's service only family gathered at his grave.
My father was present, also, and the small group waited uneasily
for the volunteer pastor who never appeared.
The assassin's mother finally approached my father,
asking if he would say at least a few words about her son.
I wasn't there, so I don't know if my father wavered momentarily,
but in the end he did what he believed was right.
He talked briefly with her, stepped up and read the 23rd Psalm,
and then spoke a few words about a mother's pain for her son.

Later I asked him how he could speak at the grave of the man
who had shot and killed our president?
My father's response?
It was the Christian thing to do.

Rather than life beginning to settle down,
the air in our house suddenly seemed to hold its breath.
Our phone started ringing regularly and persistently.
My parents spoke in hushed tones and usually behind closed doors.
Then came my father's announcement to my brother and me
that we would be leaving Fort Worth,
leaving our school, our church, our friends.

The calls that continued to interrupt our evenings, our lives
were death threats aimed at my father, at his family,
and they could no longer be ignored.

We made a midnight move to Dallas.
My father found a church, my parents bought a home,
and we all started over.
The balloons of anger gradually deflated in the two Texas cities
most associated with Kennedy's and Oswald's names.
If I could not fully grasp my father's reason at the time,
I was able to embrace it later.

My father was right in his decision to speak at Oswald's funeral
although the aftermath took a great toll on him—and on us.
For him it was the Christian thing to do.

Karen's Story: Journeys From and Toward

Some people speak
of walking on eggshells around difficult spouses.
That was not my experience.
For years I felt I was stepping lightly
on shards of glass and absorbing the pain.
I would have fared better with eggshells;
they would have left less scarring.

New wounds layered on top of old wounds.
The combined tissue may have toughened me,
but it also hardened me, often hindered me
from reaching the peace my mind and spirit craved.

In yoga I practice with ahimsa,
the discipline of doing no harm.
Yet I would return home to a narcissist,
a person so self-absorbed and centered on his own being
that he had no room to truly include others.

My three sons now mostly raised
and no longer living at home,
I decided it was my turn to leave.
The journey of change continues to evolve,
but I can tell you that in living alone
I am discovering new rhythms,
I am finding my breath.

Betty's Story: Clearing Off the Closet Shelf

One year my husband Roger signed up for a class
taught in our retirement community clubhouse.
He said it was called "Memoir writing"
and it would count for three hours of college credit.
Why he wanted college credit, he being almost eighty,
was beyond me and I told him so.

When the next year approached Roger nagged me
to join him and give the class a try.
I finally decided doing so would make him easier to live with
so I showed up on the first day.

One of the first things I did was raise my hand
before the professor even got started.
I am not a dyed redhead for nothing.

I then asked in my loud voice,
"What happens if a person can't get to the memories
to write about them?"

Roger mumbled, "Oh geez,"
but the teacher didn't act like my question
was inappropriate or out of order.
She even smiled.
She began by suggesting that I close my eyes
and imagine the top shelf of my closet.

Well, I don't know about anyone else,
but I'd rather not think about what's on that shelf.
Still I decided to play the game.

"Now," the teacher continued,
"you can easily see what's lining up the front of the shelf.
Right?" she nodded encouragingly.
Wanting to give the correct answer, I nodded back.
She seemed so sincere.

"But to see what is behind the first row
of items," she went on,
"you have to take them off the shelf—
or at least move them around—
to discover perhaps some treasures

94

you had forgotten about.
And then behind *them* may be other mementos
that you can't see because of all the clutter."

I was beginning to get her point.
I couldn't get to the older memories
because they were stuck behind newer ones.

Long story short, I remained in the class
and continued another four years
until the professor stopped teaching it.
And I was able to write something for every assignment.

Some memory stories were easy to write about,
enjoyable even, because they allowed me to relive
good times that somehow I managed to let escape.
Others I had to grind my teeth to get through them
and they cost me some restless nights.
But I toughed those out because we learned
to honor all the memories—good and bad—
and leave them in their rightful places.

Margo's Story: All the Music

I always took pride in keeping a clean house,
especially while the children were growing up
and even past that time—when I was still vital.
I left that house some years back
and now live among many people much like myself,
people whose minds have grown frail.

I prefer to sit at the same table in this dining room.
Two other women sit there, too, their faces finally familiar,
their names, though, meaning nothing.
After meals I spread my wide hands to press out
any wrinkles remaining in the tablecloth
because I so like a cloth to be pressed and clean.
It tells much about a good homemaker.

Someone once asked me, while watching my hands and fingers
glide across the now pressed cloth
if I used to play the piano.

"Sweetheart," I answered, "I don't know. I don't remember much."
"I think perhaps you did," she responded smiling,
still watching my hands in earnest movement.
I said nothing as my arthritic fingers paused in sweeping.

Sometimes, when I close my tired eyes,
sinking into the gentle, soothing darkness,
I'm certain I hear fragments of melodies:
clear notes that lilt and drop,
teasing me into old times.
But now I feel weary
as I strain to recall a piano.
I have listened to all the music I want to hear.

Ruth's Story: My Name

My real name was Ruth.
I was not an alcoholic,
I was not a drug addict.
What I used to be was an abused wife.

It stopped after my husband held a gun to my head—
all because I was studying for an English final
and he felt threatened that I wanted to better myself,
perhaps be more than he was.

I never made it to my English final that next morning.
Instead a stranger led me to a women's shelter.
A few months later I was taken up north,
leaving all I knew and had behind.
Even my dog.
That was fifteen years ago.

My name could no longer be Ruth.
As my husband became more computer savvy,
more persistent in searching for me,
it became necessary to change my identity,
get a new social security card,
move yet again.

I began taking college courses once more
and continued to explore my thoughts in writing.
I have filled many notebooks by now.
My life. Written down.

I was told that statistically I shouldn't be alive.
Four hours of holding a gun to my head
and knocking back cans of Schlitz,
my husband's arm finally tired,
and I got away.

Inside I am still Ruth sometimes,
wondering how on earth the dream of an education
could put my life on the line.

Threatened. Rescued. Saved.

But here I am today.
My name was Ruth.
I am a survivor.

Hester's Story: Hard Times

I was a child during the Thirties
and those years defined my girlhood
in a number of ways.

I walked to school each day—
no matter the time of year—
and often I was scolded for my dawdling.
Understand that I was a curious child
who welcomed distractions along the way.

I must have been around twelve
when I came upon the dead body.
That particular day I recall skipping along
the railroad tracks that ran for miles and miles,
picking wildflowers to take home to Mama.

I saw the torso first.
It was coverall-clad and one boot was missing.
The head lay a few feet away
resting in a patch of springtime verbena.
The eyes were open and vacant,
and that image has stayed with me ever since.
I stood still for several minutes before bolting
for the shortest route home to find my father.

Later I heard the dead man was probably a train hopper,
someone out of work and hopping trains from place to place,
seeking employment and a better chance at life.
The townies called these men hoboes
and often drew the word out with a sneer.
Easy for them to say with a swagger.
Their fathers already had jobs and put enough food on the table.

I still think about that poor soul from time to time.
No one ever learned what happened—
maybe he had had too much of the drink, as we used to say,
and simply fallen asleep on the track.

Train hopper or hobo:
It seems to me a human life is still a human life,
no matter how it is labeled.

Areza's Story: Observations on an Arranged Marriage

As a young female growing up in Pakistan
I was aware what love marriage was.
I just did not get to experience it.

During my teen years in Karachi women were just beginning
to break long-held stereotypes,
yet most families still followed a patriarchal society,
my family among them.

At twenty I became engaged to a man my parents chose for me.
It did not matter that I secretly yearned
for someone tall, dark, and handsome.
I was introduced instead to an older man—
short, squat, and balding—
and informed that he would become my life mate.

My parents were amply pleased with their decision,
and if they noticed I was quiet and trembling,
they certainly never let on.
It was not my place to question or doubt
what they considered to be in my best interest,
and it was only small consolation that my siblings
would fare the same when it came their turn.

While not in love with him,
I did in time come to love my husband.
He was kind, respectful, progressive for a Pakistani male.
Later, when our two children were still quite young,
we left the growing unrest in our country and moved to the U.S.
where prospects in his field of medicine were more favorable.

He did not require me to continue wearing the shalwar kameez
and the dupatta long native to our heritage.
Soon I adopted the westernized preferences for jeans and tops,
appreciating that my husband understood my desire
for assimilation while attending college classes,
welcoming his support as I pursued a degree.

Today I note the popularity of romance fiction,
I listen to couples sigh that the "honeymoon phase" has ended,
and I think perhaps it is the many expectations
that lead to inevitable disappointments.

It is then that I revisit my reluctance sixteen years earlier
when my parents pronounced me engaged.
In the weeks before my wedding
they taught me that commitment to making a marriage work
comes first, in equal measures from both partners.
Personal feelings and needs come second.
All together they produce fullness.

Mary Jean's Story: Not a Crusader but a Helping Hand

Dallas in the Sixties acted all progressive,
but that really wasn't exactly so.
I lived in the north end of the city where streets
were more consistently repaired and maintained
and the city pools were kept updated and clean
since they were populated by white folks.

The south end of the city told a different story,
one that never set well with me.
Church friends and the like considered me quirky,
and more than several dubbed me "the Crusader"
since I drove down to areas they never would have dared,
helping out where I could.

I often treated siblings to fast-food burgers, chocolate malts,
not caring I was the only white person in the place,
my attention drawn to the children's obvious pleasure
of sitting in a booth, smearing French fries in catsup
and basking in the refrigerated air which their homes lacked.

Other times I would prepare a picnic lunch,
drive downtown to the Center where I was known,
and drive back northwest with a carful of wiggling bodies
to a lake where the kids could feed the ducks
and watch the planes fly over the water, the engines
rumbling loud and close, causing squeals and hand-covered ears.

I volunteered my time and heart during hot summers
while friends were playing bridge and trading gossip,
each of us choosing the pastime that satisfied our needs.

But I resisted their well-intentioned description
of me as a south city crusader when I saw myself
far more truthfully as simply a helping hand living more fully,
connecting with lives different from my own.

Tiffany's Story: Becoming

I clearly recall my first college class,
remember being a thirty-five-year-old in the midst
of the innocence and energy of eighteen-year-olds.
I, too, had planned to go to college at their age.
Instead I married and had a baby.
And then another several years later.
Now with my youngest at last in kindergarten,
I decided it was my turn.
It seemed like a bold adventure at the time of registration,
but then I hadn't factored in the years I had been out of school—
until that very first day of my first semester.
My five-year-old probably had fared better on his first day.

My mind drifted frequently that first morning
as I absorbed my surroundings.
When I tuned back in, the professor was at the board
and I heard the words "grammar review."
Had I been sitting on the other side of the room—
by the door—
I might have bailed.
Grammar review in college?
Yikes!

Thus began my initiation into the realm of Higher Ed.
I sucked in my breath recalling my long-planned decision.
Wasn't I here to be challenged?
Didn't I want to continue to learn?
Hadn't I been wanting to be more?

I was indeed challenged.
The grade of C on my first essay stung.
The professor's marks on the pages resembled puncture wounds.
Later I would realize it was my pride that had been wounded.
My essay deserved the C.

These twelve years later,
I'm glad I wasn't sitting near the door that morning.
What a loss it would have been to bail
when I have become so much more.
Now a teacher myself, I continue to acquire more confidence
as I hone the skills I bring to my classroom.
I count the triumphs of mastery in areas once foreign to me,

once unnerving—such as the semicolon.
Not long ago I was intimidated by it;
now I am infatuated with it.

Irma's Story: Unexpected Turns

I grew up in the Piney Woods of East Texas,
running barefoot most of the year,
wearing hand-me-down shoes in the winter.
We were money-poor, that was a fact,
but my siblings and I were rich in curiosity
and taught by our mother to read early-on.

Upon graduating high school my brother went west
to work in the oil fields and ended up staying.
My sister married a local boy and set up house.
I had hopes of going to college in a big city,
but then the Second World War commenced
and the country seemed to turn topsy-turvy.
I stayed home, found a job at the Dry Goods store,
and signed up for a correspondence course in typing.
Next I enrolled in an accounting course.
I had not lost my aptitude for learning.

One day I saw a notice in the Sulphur Springs paper
posting a location and date for taking the civil service exam.
I was twenty by then, restless and ready to escape
the confines of small town life,
the stirrings of gumption no longer dormant.

Oh my, what a twist my life took after that bus ride
into the city and then to the government building.
My test score arrived in the mail with a question attached:
Would I be interested in coming to D.C. for an interview?
The position would a require a security clearance.

It was then 1943.
I began my job in Intelligence and remained in D.C.
for the duration of the war.
And that is all I am going to say about that.

Annie's Story: Hardscrabble Honeymoon

Daughter of a sheep man and a true pioneer mother
who bore ten children and outlived half of them,
I grew up in the small town of Sherwood, Texas
where rainfall was scant but there was, nonetheless,
a little creek with live oaks and cedars for shade.
By no means did we have an easy life,
but it was the life we had and knew—
about the same as most folks around.

When I became a young woman I met Frank,
who was helping out at his uncle's sheep camp.
Good-looking and with a head of thick wavy hair,
he appeared to fancy me and thus began our courtship.

My father made no pretense of his feelings about Frank—
probably believing my suitor lacked sufficient ambition—
and he made sure to tell me so.
Still I married Frank anyway,
the two of us traveling to San Angelo buggy-style.

I wasn't sure what a bride was supposed to expect or feel
at that time, it being the end of the frontier era,
but our honeymoon, when we returned,
was spent at the sheep camp—without even a tent—
just simply a mattress and springs under the stars.
And not especially private.

It fit the life we had and knew.
It was our hardscrabble honeymoon.

My Mother Madgie's Story: My Husband's Disappearance

I lived with a man for sixty-six years,
an earnest man with west Texas roots,
and one day he disappeared.
I looked for him behind me.
I looked for him in corners.
I looked for him in bed where he would spoon
and wrap his weakened arms around me.

I wanted him to appear, to share a table with me,
to touch my face, touch our hands.

Instead, a familiar stranger would come,
rub my hands and arms with lavender lotion,
murmur unintelligible sounds that soothed and calmed me.
Her dark doe eyes looked much like my husband's,
and I would stare into them until she slipped away
to return some other time.

I lived with a man for sixty-six years
and one day he disappeared.
At long last I decided to find him.
I pulled at the air as if it were a veil,
as if he were standing behind it
in the gauze of pale light,
in the lingering scent of lavender.

CPSIA information can be obtained
at www.ICGtesting.com
Printed in the USA
BVHW040835270522
638300BV00006B/158